Millionaire Mindset

Transforming Your Approach to Wealth

Table of Contents

Chapter 1. Introduction

Delve into the world of opulence with our dynamic Special Report, "Millionaire Mindset: Transforming Your Approach to Wealth". This enlightening read isn't just about numbers and strategies; it's about cultivating a paradigm shift in how you perceive and generate wealth. Rooted in the lives and habits of self-made millionaires, this report uncovers the philosophies and tactics that can empower you to take that exciting journey towards financial freedom. Embark on this transformative expedition and discover what it truly means to think like a millionaire. Every slice of wisdom packed in these pages could be your golden ticket to the world you've dreamed of. Don't just chase wealth – understand it, control it, and cultivate it! Start transforming your mindset today for a prosperous tomorrow. This report might just be your first step towards your millionaire journey. Dive in and start writing your success story today!

Chapter 2. The Origins of the Millionaire Mindset

The millionaire mindset didn't evolve by accident, nor did it come about overnight. The origins of the millionaire mindset can be traced back through history, examining the lives of self-made millionaires and distilling the perspectives, principles, and strategies that have contributed to their vast fortunes.

2.1. The Wealth Philosophy

Wealth, as perceived by the millionaire, is not merely a store of money. It's an embodiment of freedom, security, possibilities, influence, and impact. The millionaire mindset originated as a philosophy that sought balance between material accumulation and personal growth. Millionaires' pursuit of wealth was always tied to a larger vision rather than focusing solely on immediate material gratification.

2.2. The Birth Of Autonomy

Among the earliest instances of this mindset, we find merchants and traders. In societies dominated by feudal lords, they embodied the spirit of autonomy and enterprise. These early wealth creators recognized the importance of taking calculated risks, actively seeking opportunities, and investing in their pursuits. This framework of thinking marked the beginning of what we now call the entrepreneurial mindset.

Their spirit of autonomy and enterprise helped create a capitalist economy, shifting power away from landed nobles to individuals who created wealth through trade and innovation. This was the bedrock upon which the millionaire mindset was built.

2.3. The Role of Innovation

With the advent of the industrial revolution, the millionaire mindset took on a new dimension: innovation. Inventors, scientists, and entrepreneurs broke ground with revolutionary technologies, industry-altering strategies, and market-creating value propositions. Wealth creation was no longer just about trade; it was about disrupting industries and crafting new rules of play.

The likes of Andrew Carnegie, Cornelius Vanderbilt, and John D. Rockefeller exemplified this attitude. They embraced innovation as a path to wealth, investing in technologies and industries that reshaped our world. These men understood that wealth accumulation is synergistic with progress, leading to greater prosperity for society.

Their pursuit of innovation still reverberates in today's millionaire mindset. The belief in creating value, disrupting markets, and welcoming change is strong in today's self-made millionaires.

=== Mindset Over Money

However, the millionaire mindset isn't limited to the pursuit of business success. Early philosophers and thinkers contributed significantly to shaping the millionaire mindset by instilling the importance of personal development and continuous learning.

Foremost among them was Benjamin Franklin. While known for his inventions and political contributions, he was also one of the earliest proponents of the self-made ideal and the embodiment of the American Dream. His thirteen virtues of self-improvement - including industry, frugality, and sincerity – indicate the importance placed on intrinsic qualities over material accumulation. This echoes strongly in the mindset of the majority of millionaires today.

Chapter 3. A Legacy That Lives On

From these humble beginnings, the millionaire mindset has evolved into a sophisticated framework for thinking about wealth, success, and personal growth. Yet, the core principles remain the same: autonomy, innovation, continuous learning, and personal development. It's these principles that have guided successful millionaires for centuries and continue to form the basis of the millionaire mindset today.

Whether it's creating new technologies, running large corporations, starting a small business, or investing in stocks, the millionaire mindset underpins all these activities. It allows for the immense wealth, freedom, and impact that being a millionaire can bring.

As we delve into the lives and habits of self-made millionaires, the millionaire mindset begins to unfold. It shows us how ordinary people with extraordinary mindsets can achieve what most people only dream of. It's a journey of personal growth and transformation, and it starts with understanding its origins and how it came to be. As we revisit the back alleys and brightly lit boardrooms of history, we discover the recurring narrative: wealth is an outward manifestation of the inner millionaire mindset. We start to understand that wealth isn't about what you have – it's about who you become.

Today, the notion of the 'millionaire' is not limited to the monetary value itself. It has taken on a greater meaning, symbolizing freedom, security, achievement, and even philanthropy. Every era has its millionaires, each reflecting their time's opportunities, challenges, and values. But the inner millionaire mindset, with its insatiable curiosity, obsession with improvement, love of independence, and bold ambition, remains much the same – it is timeless.

Chapter 4. Embracing the Wealth-Driven Lifestyle

The path to abundant prosperity isn't purely a financial route. Rather, it's a lifestyle adjustment that demands a mental shift from surviving to thriving, an acceptance of thinking big, and a desire to make wealth a central part of life. Embracing a wealth-driven lifestyle involves stepping out of comfort zones, making careful choices, developing productive habits, and nurturing specific attitudes.

4.1. Crafting a Wealth Consciousness

One cannot understate the importance of mindset in the journey towards wealth. Almost without exception, self-made millionaires possess a 'wealth consciousness' - a belief in the plenitude of the universe and surety in their ability to partake in that abundance. To foster this consciousness, one must repeatedly visualize wealth, success, and opulence, thereby acknowledging and embracing their financial desires completely.

Creating a mental picture of success helps reaffirm belief in one's goals. Visualization embodies the future, forming the trajectory to achieving it. Devote time each day to sitting in tranquil reflection contemplating life as a millionaire, imagining the liberation of financial freedom and the luxurious comforts that accompany wealth.

4.2. The Power of Affirmation

By coupling visualization with affirmations, one reinforces the wealth consciousness. Affirmations are positive assertions spoken with conviction. They cater to the subconscious mind, building self-confidence and strengthening the belief in one's potential to amass wealth.

Starting each day with wealth-inspired affirmations such as "I have a millionaire mindset", "Wealth flows easily into my life", and "I create abundance effortlessly" has incalculably positive impacts. What might seem like a simple exercise can cultivate a sense of empowerment and focus, guiding all actions towards wealth creation.

4.3. Value Driven Life

Wealth isn't merely accumulation; it's the vehicle that translates values into tangible reality. A million-pound bank statement isn't the end goal; it's the potential to actualize life in a way that authentically reflects one's values and passions. Recognizing this solidifies the commitment to wealth creation.

Consider listing out the things that truly matter. What will financial emancipation enable of these? This could range from maintaining a high standard of living, providing a secure future for your family, contributing to charitable causes, or just having the freedom to experience the finer things in life. These core motivations form the backbone of the wealth-driven lifestyle.

4.4. The Millionaire Morning Ritual

```
[table]
|===
| Hours
| Activities
```

```
| 5:00 ⎯ 6:00
```

| Fitness / Exercise

| 6:00 – 7:00
| Visioning / Affirmation / Visualization

| 7:00 – 8:00
| Personal development Reading / Learning

| 8:00 – 9:00
| Planning / Prioritizing the Day's Activities
|===

Beginning the day on a high note sets the tone for the following hours. Follow a structured morning routine focused on personal growth and goal alignment. Physical exercise for health, visualization for mindset molding, reading for knowledge acquisition, and planning for productivity can contribute to a fruitful day aligning the lifestyle to wealth accumulation.

4.5. Setting Wealth Goals

Creating monetary targets breaches a taboo threshold, moving aims from abstract to concrete. Explicit goals encourage strategic planning, ensuring actions align with broader wealth objectives. The act of writing out these goals magnetizes them, pulling towards reality the desired financial outcomes.

Establish one-year, five-year, and ten-year wealth goals. Assess them regularly, celebrating achievements and adjusting plans as needed. This practice nurtures a sense of ownership towards wealth creation and affords discoverable paths to desired results.

4.6. Continuous Learning and Skill Enhancement

Intellectual property goes a long way in wealth creation. The digital era has opened myriad avenues for skill learning and knowledge acquisition. Online courses, webinars, podcasts, and books abound, offering rich resources to sharpen skills and stay informed about financial trends and strategies.

Actively seek learning opportunities, focussing on finance, entrepreneurship, investment, and personal development. In an economy driven by intellectual capital, a continuous learning mindset is a valuable asset for any wealth-creator.

Embracing a wealth-driven lifestyle is a multifaceted process that surpasses just adopting investment strategies or financial planning. It permeates every aspect of life, shaping choices, and underpinning habits. The successful millionaire deeds each day to wealth creation and prosperity, fostering a deep-seated belief in their deservedness of life's abundance, and working relentlessly to actualize it. And in this relentless pursuit, lies the crux of the journey from scarcity to abundance.

Chapter 5. Pathways to Prosperity: Revisiting Your Financial Goals

Far too often, people think about wealth as a dollar figure - a certain amount of money in the bank; a certain luxury car; a specific kind of house. However, true wealth transcends material possessions. It involves a sense of prosperity and well-being in all areas of life, rooted in freedom, independence, and a long-term vision. Embracing this broader vision of wealth is the first step on the pathway to prosperity.

5.1. Transform Your Vision

To create your pathway to prosperity, start by transforming your vision of what wealth means. Don't trap yourself in the idea that wealth is only about a specific figure. Instead, think about what financial freedom means to you - perhaps it means the ability to travel the world without worrying about expenses; the capability to provide for your family without financial stress; the opportunity to pursue the hobbies and activities that bring you joy; or the independence to follow your dreams without getting stuck in a 9-5 routine.

5.2. Set Your Financial Goals

An integral part of your journey is goal setting. Without clear, defined motivations, even the greatest intentions can flounder. Whether it's eliminating debt, investing in real estate, or planning your retirement, each journey to wealth begins with a goal. While setting these goals, keep the SMART (Specific, Measurable, Achievable, Relevant, and Time-bound) criteria in mind.

Furthermore, consider your lifestyle, family, and personal circumstances. Goals that are not in sync with these aspects are bound to be deserted mid-way.

5.3. Build Your Financial Roadmap

With your financial goals defined, it's now time to create a roadmap. Your financial roadmap should represent the tactical steps you need to achieve your broader vision. It's a flexible, evolving tool that details your savings, investments, expenditures, and other financial decisions. Review it periodically and readjust as necessary to keep pace with changes in your personal circumstances or financial environment.

5.4. Understand Your Financial Personality

Attaining financial freedom requires an understanding of your financial personality. This process involves noticing your attitudes, beliefs, emotions, and behaviors around money. Some people are savers, others are spenders; some are risk-averse, while others thrive on financial risk. By understanding your money personality, you can tailor a financial strategy that aligns with your natural tendencies.

5.5. Develop Wealth-Building Habits

As you continue this journey, cultivate the habits that fuel wealth creation. Millionaires understand that wealth creation results from consistent, strategic habits, among them careful budgeting, thoughtful investing, continuous learning, and the habit of giving.

Firstly, budgeting isn't about being miserly. It's about knowing where your money goes and making conscious decisions on how you want to use it.

Secondly, investing is more than just buying stocks on a whim. It's about understanding market trends, diversifying your portfolio to spread risk, and adopting a long-term investing outlook.

Continuous learning is another cornerstone habit. To stay updated with the latest market trends, investment strategies, and financial innovations, you must adopt a learning mindset, becoming a student of your own financial growth.

Lastly, the habit of giving, which might seem counterintuitive in a wealth-creation strategy, is central to many millionaire mindsets. Philanthropy doesn't only benefit the recipient, but also the donor, encouraging a mindset of abundance, attracting greater wealth, happiness, and prosperity.

Every detail in this wealth-creation journey matters - from every decision made, every risk taken, and every goal set. In this transformative journey of turning vision into reality, every step matters. And each step can become a transformational shift towards your path to prosperity. Keep going, keep learning, and keep enriching your millionaire mindset. Who knows, your first million might be closer than you think.

Chapter 6. Garnering Growth: Creativity and Innovation in Wealth Creation

The engine of wealth creation hums with the power of creativity and innovation. For the self-made millionaire, these are no mere abstract concepts, but the essential tools that empower them to step beyond the ordinary people living ordinary lives into the realm of the extraordinary. Harnessed correctly, creativity and innovation become the driving forces behind unprecedented wealth creation, providing solutions to problems, new products for markets, and efficiencies within industries.

6.1. Cultivating a Creative Mindset

Before embarking on the path of wealth creation, one essential step is to cultivate a creative mindset. This involves breaking free from typical thinking patterns and being open to new ideas, embracing change, looking at problems as opportunities, and acquiring the courage to take risks.

Bruce Lee once said, "The usefulness of a cup is its emptiness." To capture the essence of creativity, you must let go of preconceived theories, ideas, and biases. Like an empty cup, only when the mind is devoid of these blockages can it fill up with fresh, innovative, and exciting thoughts. This unlearning of known concepts is often the first phase of nurturing creativity that paves the way for wealth creation.

Creativity can be compared to a muscle that needs regular exercise to keep fit. The daily routine of solving puzzles, studying art, learning musical instruments, or just spending time in nature can stimulate the process of creative thinking. Furthermore, an individual needs to maintain an insatiable curiosity, questioning every aspect around them to feed their creative mind.

6.2. Converting Creativity into Innovation

While creativity is all about generating original ideas, innovation refers to the practical application of these ideas into tangible value-creating concepts. Here lies the true essence of wealth creation. You need to create a sense of balance between imagination and reality, where you visualize ideas with a creative mind and land them in the realm of applicability via innovation.

The main ingredient in this mix is the power of observation. The most innovative of people are adept at spotting potential opportunities camouflaged as problems. They convert these problems into projects, transforming them into income-generating enterprises. In this context, one must understand the marketplace, acknowledge its needs, and develop a knack for sensing the upcoming trends and shifts before they're visible to the masses.

6.3. Developing an Entrepreneurial Spirit

An entrepreneurial spirit is a mindset that seeks out change rather than waiting to adapt to it. It empowers you to take the lead, embrace challenges, and construct a path of success that is uniquely yours. This mindset is the critical element that enables the transition of creative ideas into innovative, wealth-generating enterprises.

Entrepreneurs dare to dream, but their dreams are fuelled by calculated risks rather than airy hopes. They are voracious learners, persistent in their pursuits, and resilient in the face of failure. When faced with adversity, they see not a dead end but a detour taking them one step closer to their goal.

Entrepreneurship is not an innate skill; rather, it is cultivated and honed over time. By adopting the right attitude and continuous learning, this critical tool can be developed, which is essential for escalating the ladder of wealth creation.

6.4. Employing Innovation and Creativity in the Age of Digital Transformation

In this age of rapid digital transformation, the twin forces of creativity and innovation offer vast, untapped potential for wealth creation. New-age millionaires are harnessing these strengths, providing novel solutions to longstanding problems, and reaping immense financial rewards in the process.

From e-commerce to fintech solutions, Artificial Intelligence to Blockchain, progressive innovations are shaping the landscape of wealth creation. Ingenious entrepreneurs are leveraging these cutting-edge technologies, reimagining the ways we conduct business, spend money or save it – even how we interact with the world around us.

Creativity and innovation, when powered by digital technology, create a formidable force that drives wealth generation at an unprecedented scale. The digital realm offers an expansive playground full of opportunities for the innovatively inclined.

In conclusion, harnessing creativity and innovation can lead to remarkable growth in wealth creation. But embarking on this journey requires a shift in mindset — one that breaks free from the stereotypical thought processes, sees opportunities in difficulties, and values the power of dreaming big. It necessitates a playground where ideas are planted like seeds, nourished and fostered to bloom into the fruit-bearing trees of wealth creation. This journey may be challenging, but it is undeniably rewarding and has the potential to create a ripple effect of prosperity that extends well beyond individual success to positively impact the broader community and indeed, the world.

Chapter 7. Risk and Reward: Essential Factors in Building Great Fortunes

One of the most pivotal components in the realm of financial prosperity is the balance between risk and reward – a dance that, if completed with precision and understanding, can turn seemingly ordinary ventures into generators of astounding profit. It's by mastering the nuances of this relationship that everyday people metamorphosize into self-made millionaires.

7.1. Understanding Risk and Reward

At their core, risk and reward are two sides of the same coin. Risk signifies the potential for loss, and reward, on the other hand, represents the potential gain. The likelihood of considerable rewards often walks hand in hand with significant risks. In the context of investments, high risk usually equates to high returns, and low risk typically means moderate returns.

To illustrate, consider a savings account, a low-risk investment. It provides a minimal return, often merely sufficient to keep pace with inflation. In contrast, equities or stocks, which are high-risk investments, can yield exponential growth.

Navigating this balance of risk and reward, then, pivots predominantly on how well an individual comprehends the nature of the venture and how effectively they can weigh the odds of both profit and loss.

7.2. Prudent Risk Taking: The Millionaire's Approach

So, how do self-made millionaires approach risk-taking? First, understand that risk doesn't deter them. Instead, they make calculated moves, well-aware of the fact that fortune favors the bold but only when coupled with informed decision-making.

Take, for example, investing in the stock market. It is an uncertain terrain, notorious for its volatility. Average investors might shy away from it, preferring the safety of low-yield bonds or fixed deposits. Millionaires, however, see beyond the immediate turbulence. They formulate investment strategies that factor in statistical data, market trends, and company fundamentals. They understand that while the stock market is unpredictable, it's also one of the most rewarding playgrounds for building substantial wealth over time.

They also accept that failures and setbacks are part of the journey. Rather than being paralyzed by an ill-fated venture, they learn from it, recoup, and strategize their next move with enhanced wisdom. Every failure can fertilize the soil for future success, provided one knows how to cultivate valuable lessons from the experience.

7.3. The Art of Diversification

Risk management doesn't mean avoiding risk entirely but rather distributing your risk. Putting all of your eggs in one basket is a risky proposition. Instead, spread them out over a wide field where they can grow and multiply - this is the essence of diversification. Self-made millionaires exercise diversification not just across industries and asset classes but also on a global scale.

Taking a diversified approach not only protects against catastrophic losses, but it also opens up multiple channels of potential profitability. For an individual holding numerous investments, should one falter, it's probable another one's performing well, meaning your portfolio can stay buoyant. Diversification operates as your portfolio's safety net, reducing risk while securing potential rewards.

7.4. Patience: The Silent Ingredient in Wealth Creation

Another crucial point to consider in the risk-reward paradigm is the aspect of patience. Time plays an essential role here. The alluring stories of overnight successes are often outliers, not norms. Millionaires understand that sustained wealth creation demands patience and consistency.

Consider, for example, the concept of compounding. Consistently investing over a long period allows your wealth to grow exponentially rather than linearly. As illustrated by such tales as Warren Buffett (who is said to have made 99% of his wealth after his 50th birthday), patience can be an extremely profitable strategy when aligned with intelligent risk-taking and effective diversification. In essence, the magic trio of compounding returns - time, rate, and principal - can weave wonders given a conducive stage.

With this chapter's wisdom, we hope you can navigate the treacherous yet tantalizing path of risks and rewards more comfortably. Remember that there's no one-size-fits-all approach, it all comes down to your personal comfort with risk, financial goals, and time horizon. If you can put fear aside and embrace prudent, intelligent risk-taking, who's to say you won't be the next self-made millionaire success story?

Chapter 8. Unlocking Financial Discipline: Millionaire Spending Habits

Financial discipline is a cornerstone in the foundation of wealth, and millionaires may exemplify this more than anyone else. Contrary to the extravagant lifestyles often portrayed in the media, many millionaires practice a level of frugality and discipline, which allowed them to accumulate their wealth in the first place.

8.1. Frugality: The Unsung Hero of Wealth Accumulation

Becoming a millionaire doesn't necessarily mean indulging in expensive habits. In fact, it often means the opposite — frugality. Being frugal isn't about being cheap, but making the most out of what you have and ensuring that each dollar or cent is spent wisely.

Being frugal is about differentiating between needs and wants, and prioritizing spending based on this. While this does not suggest that millionaires never spend on luxuries, they ensure to address their needs first. This habit not only applies to personal spending but also extends to investments and long-term financial plans, forging a path towards affluent growth.

8.2. Understanding and Utilizing Assets

One's perception of wealth greatly influences their spending habits. Millionaires perceive wealth as an endowment of assets rather than a hoard of money.

Are assets just bulky properties, lucrative business deals, or towering stocks? For millionaires, assets go beyond these tangible entities. Time, skills, knowledge, relationships, even good health are seen as valuable assets. Herein, lies the profound difference. Millionaires continually invest in these assets to augment their wealth, aligning all expenses to contribute to their asset pool, ensuring a continuous stream of income independent of their direct labor.

Just as crucial as accumulating assets, is the need for protecting them. An important aspect of millionaire spending habits is the appropriation of funds to insurance plans and legal protection schemes. These protect their assets from unforeseen conditions and uncertainties.

8.3. The Millionaire's Demystification of Debts

Debts often lure people into a vicious cycle, but millionaires have a different relationship with debt. They understand the subtle difference between good debts and bad debts, and they wisely use good debts to their advantage.

A 'good debt' refers to borrowing money for investments that grow in value or generate long-term income. On the contrary, 'bad debts' are those that do not increase value or generate income.

Millionaires control their debts instead of letting the debts control them. They make careful calculations, projecting the income from the borrowed money against the interest it accrues. If the projected income outweighs the interest, they'll consider the debt – tying back to the earlier point about each cent being spent wisely.

8.4. Budgeting & Planning: The Blueprint of Financial Security

Every millionaire understands the power of a well-planned budget. A budget is a roadmap that guides spending and savings to achieve financial goals. Most millionaires strictly adhere to this budget and constantly review and adjust it to fit their ever-evolving financial landscape.

With a clearly outlined budget backed by research and a careful understanding of market trends, millionaires can easily keep their spending habits in check.

8.5. Making Investments Work: A Hands-on Approach

Millionaires recognise the potential of investments to generate wealth. However, they do not simply throw money blindly into investments; they take a hands-on approach, making a conscious decision wherever their money goes.

They leverage investment opportunities in ways that best meet their risk tolerance, return expectations and personal knowledge.

Investments, when managed correctly, provide continuous cash flow without directly trading time for money, enabling millionaires to maintain or even improve their current lifestyle without dipping into their savings.

8.6. The Emblem of Charity: Giving Money a Purpose

Most of the world's millionaires are philanthropists at heart. Giving back to society is a notable part of their financial landscape.

Charitable contributions offer a deeper perspective on money, spreading wealth beyond their personal sphere and promoting a sense of purpose and fulfillment, which inspires them to make more.

8.7. The Power of Continuous Learning

Finally, the most affluent individuals constantly seek knowledge on how to better manage their wealth. They commit to lifelong learning, seeking expert guidance, reading widely, and attending financial seminars. By staying informed of financial principles, trends, and strategies, they can maintain their wealth over time.

In a nutshell, understanding the millionaire mindset and embracing their financial discipline is the first step towards experiencing a shift in your financial situation. Wealth creation isn't about uncontrolled spending; on the contrary, it is about discipline, budgeting, controlling debts, investing wisely, and giving generously. Understand, control, and cultivate wealth. This is the millionaire way.

Chapter 9. Powerful Investment Strategies of Millionaires

Investment strategies may seem daunting, yet millionaires have often tread these paths, with meticulous planning and understanding as their guides. Their tactics are as diverse as they are smart; they explore a broad range of investment opportunities, think ahead and stay adaptive to market fluctuations. Be it real estate, stocks, or business investments; they probe, ponder, and invest wisely.

9.1. Diversification of Portfolio

No journey to riches starts or continues unabated without recognizing the importance of portfolio diversification. The wealthiest understand that putting all eggs in one basket isn't the surest strategy to manage and multiply wealth. Effective diversification necessitates an understanding of different investment fields, whether it be stocks, bonds, real estate, businesses, or more modern ventures like cryptocurrencies.

Efficient diversification isn't achieved by merely owning a variety any type of assets, but by selecting investments that yield good returns and don't rise and fall together. A diversified portfolio absorbs shocks and delivers steady long-term returns. Millionaires, therefore, endeavor to understand varying markets, trends and make informed decisions about where to spread their net.

9.2. Prudent Risk Management

Millionaires understand that investments carry inherent risks. Instead of shying away, they mitigate risks through intelligent strategies. They set proper risk-reward ratios, stipulate 'stop-loss' limits and don't panic in a turbulent market - they remain calm, embracing volatility as an unavoidable, yet manageable, aspect of investing.

It is important to set a risk tolerance level while investing. Millionaires typically invest only the amount of money they can afford to lose without affecting their standard of living. This doesn't mean they adopt an overly defensive approach but signals the strategic balance they strive to maintain between risk and reward.

9.3. Long-term Investment Horizon

Patience is a virtue, especially in investment strategy. Millionaires steer clear of the rapacious 'get-rich-quick' schemes. They understand wealth growth as a long-term game, marked by a strategy that compounds returns over the years. They select their investments meticulously, not swayed by momentary trends, and have an undeterred focus on long-term yields.

Long-term investments reap the benefit of compound interest, which Albert Einstein once designated as the eighth wonder of the world. He who understands it, earns it, and he who doesn't, pays it. Millionaires understand this principle and utilize it to expand their wealth.

9.4. Real Estate Investment

Real estate holds a significant position in the portfolio of many self-made millionaires, and for a good reason. It provides a resilient income source, excellent tax benefits, and potential appreciation. Real estate can serve as a stable investment that combats inflation while yielding considerable returns.

Despite occasional market downturns, home prices have consistently grown over the decades. By owning rental properties, millionaires generate a steady stream of passive income. Moreover, the tax code provisions associated with real estate are far more favorable compared to other forms of investments.

9.5. Asset Allocation Adjustments

The allocation of investments across various asset types is not a one-time decision, but rather a dynamic strategy that self-made millionaires regularly reassess and recalibrate in line with their financial goals, risk-tolerance level and market volatility. Changes in the economic climate, geopolitical situations and personal financial goals warrant adjustments in asset allocation.

Millionaires understand that as they age, their investment strategy needs revision. While it's agreeable to take risks at a younger age, as one grows older, investments should gradually be transitioned into more stable, less risky ones that ensure a safe and comfortable retirement.

9.6. Embracing New Investment Avenues

In the rapidly transforming world, staying abreast of new investment avenues is crucial. Many millionaires have garnered significant returns from investing early in future technologies like cryptocurrencies, AI and technology startups. Here, the millionaires' formula is relatively simple – explore, understand, and invest with caution.

Expanding your investment horizon involves recognizing and seizing emerging opportunities. As these opportunities multiply, due to our globally interconnected economy and technological advancement, staying informed and taking calculated risks can yield impressive results.

9.7. Continual Learning and Adaptability

Millionaires champion the power of continual learning. Regardless of their success, they remain students at heart, persistently updating their knowledge and understanding of markets, investment tools, and strategies. This adaptability extends to staying ahead of economic shifts, legislative changes, technological advancements, and global events, which could influence their investments.

Investing strategies are continually evolving, influenced by a myriad of factors. The successful millionaire mindset understands that to maintain and grow wealth, an adaptive approach is a prerequisite. This mindset of continual learning fuels an investigative spirit, constantly looking for new knowledge and innovative tactics to leverage financial trends.

Investing, like many things in life, is a journey. The millionaire investment strategies emphasized in this text may guide your path as it has for many successful people. Diversification, prudence in risk management, long-term investing, real estate, adaptability in asset allocation, embracing new investment avenues and the commitment to continual learning – these constitute the powerful investment strategies of millionaires.

However, remember that there's no one-size-fits-all strategy. It is crucial to articulate your financial goals clearly and adapt these principles accordingly. The real power of investing lies not in tips or tricks but in a clear strategy and patient, informed decisions – the ways of the millionaire mindset.

Chapter 10. The Role of Relationship Management in Wealth Accumulation

In any dialogue on wealth accumulation, our tendency is to focus on financial management, investments, and risk diversification. However, an often overlooked component that can serve as a bedrock for establishing and maintaining wealth is relationship management. The network of relationships we cultivate and the strength of our interpersonal connections can significantly impact our financial wellbeing. This chapter will delve into various aspects of relationship management and its importance in wealth accumulation.

10.1. The Power of Networking

Indeed, the old adage that 'your network is your net worth' holds quite true when it comes to wealth accumulation. Your acquaintances, friends, business associates, mentors, and even competitors could potentially open doors for you that might remain shut otherwise. These individuals not only form the basis of your network, they may also serve as investors or patrons, share useful industry knowledge or even refer potential opportunities to you. So, in essence, the quality of your relationships can influence your net worth and capacity for wealth accumulation.

10.2. Relationships with Mentors

Having a mentor in your field of interest, possessing substantial experience and credible success, can add tremendous value to your wealth accumulation process. Mentors usually have years or even decades of industry participation, and they have a vantage perspective on the failings and successes that typify the domain. Crucially, a mentor will guide you through the pitfalls and obstacles that might shackle your wealth generation efforts. In addition, a mentor can introduce you to their network, thereby offering you diverse channels to resources and opportunities.

10.3. Partnerships and Collaboration

In the realm of business, one person, notwithstanding how gifted, is unlikely to have all the necessary skills to ensure ongoing success. The world's top entrepreneurs recognize this and often cultivate strong partnerships based on mutual skills, interest, and values. Partnering with the right people, who can account for one's own deficiencies, can improve business outcomes remarkably and hasten the journey to wealth accumulation. It takes time to build these relationships, but once established, they can offer rich dividends.

10.4. Customer and Client Relationship

Understanding your customer's needs, desires, and perspectives are fundamentally imperative in fuellying your wealth accumulation journey. Excellent customer service drives customer satisfaction, fostering loyalty and referrals, which eventually boost your revenues. You must also focus on maintaining and enhancing these relationships to ensure a consistent revenue stream.

10.5. Institution-Banking Relationships

Establishing healthy relationships with your banking institution can benefit you in many ways - from favorable loan terms to advice on financial decisions. Being diligent about these relationships and keeping your personal banker informed about your needs and circumstances can mold these relationships in your favor, which in turn contributes to your wealth accumulation.

10.6. Relationship Management Practices

Now that we've established how diverse relationships contribute to wealth accumulation, it's essential to focus on some beneficial relationship management practices.

- Keeping it Professional: While personal relationships might have a bearing on partnership formation, it's important to keep business transactions strictly professional to avert unnecessary complications.

- Maintaining Open Communication: Maintaining transparency and facilitating communication ensures the reinforcement of trust, which solidifies the bonds of relationships and leads to potential opportunities.

- Being Genuine: Sincerity in any relationship invokes a feeling of trust, respect, and mutual understanding. This can be especially pivotal in business relationships, as it cultivates loyalty and long-term cooperation.

- Providing Value: In all relationships, make sure that you have something valuable to offer, be it a service, insight or support.

- Respecting Boundaries: Every relationship, particularly professional ones, require a respectful understanding of boundaries to maintain and further the relationship.

10.7. Conclusion

While financial acumen, a great business idea, and market understanding are conventionally associated with wealth generation, relationship management is an undercurrent that carries the potential to multiply that wealth manifold. With the right relationships and approach to managing them, you significantly enhance your opportunities and resources, sustaining your journey to financial prosperity. Remember, the wealthiest individuals didn't climb their mountains alone; they relied on the support, wisdom, and companionship of others.

This detailed exploration shows that the role of relationship management in wealth accumulation is dynamic, diverse, and far-reaching. Relationship management is not about manipulation for personal gains; it is about meaningful human connections that foster mutual growth and prosperity. So make it a point to invest in your relationships, nurture them, and watch how they transform your wealth accumulation journey.

Chapter 11. Multimillionaire Case Studies: Learning from Success Stories

An old phrase emphasizes, "Learn from the mistakes of others. You can't live long enough to make them all yourself." The truth is, it's equally important to learn from the success of others, especially when it comes to financial prosperity. Assessing the lives of some who have risen above the common lot, transcending from mere dreamers to multimillionaire achievers offers tremendous insights. Let's now delve into a few extraordinary stories.

11.1. The Oracle of Omaha: Warren Buffett

Considered one of the most successful investors of all time and affectionately known as the "Oracle of Omaha," Warren Buffett continues to inspire the world with his practical, yet powerful investing wisdom. Buffett's journey to his current net worth of over $100 billion began with his investment in a single business that was failing. He transformed the business's trajectory by meticulously researching his investments, focusing on enduring quality over short-term trends. Warren Buffett emphasizes the importance of understanding rather than speculating. Never invest in a business you can't comprehend, and always maintain a long-term perspective.

11.2. Self-Made Mogul: Oprah Winfrey

From an extremely challenging childhood to becoming a billionaire media executive and talk show host, Oprah Winfrey's financial success story is nothing short of incredible. Oprah's story teaches us that background and circumstances do not define our future. She worked her way up, clinching her own show, then founding Harpo Studios and OWN Network. Her success is rooted in passion, self-belief, persistence, and a determination to create value for her audience. Harnessing her personal brand proactively, Oprah diversified her revenue streams, investing in areas such as publishing and real estate.

11.3. Technology Titan: Elon Musk

Few entrepreneurs have disrupted multiple industries like Elon Musk. Known for his incredible risk-taking abilities, Musk bet his entire fortune on his companies, Tesla and SpaceX, when they were on the brink of bankruptcy during the 2008 recession. Musk pushes the boundaries of what's possible, and his vision extends beyond amassing wealth. He is driven by a mission to solve humanity's problems. Learning from Musk, it becomes evident that fearlessness in the face of adversity, a problem-solving mindset, and unwavering belief in one's vision can lead to unprecedented success.

11.4. Real Estate Rainmaker: Donald Bren

Donald Bren, the richest real-estate entrepreneur in the U.S, started with a vision of developing a master-planned community in the 1960s. Today, the property tycoon boasts an estimated $15.3 billion fortune through his real estate development company, Irvine Company. Bren's success illustrates the power of long-term strategic planning, property value appreciation, and consistent real estate transformation. His approach underscores the essence of creating value over time and leveraging opportunities in high-potential markets.

11.5. Retail Magnate: Amancio Ortega

Amancio Ortega, the notoriously private co-founder of the revolutionary fashion brand Zara, is a classic rags-to-riches tale. Ortega's journey from helping his mother clean houses to become the sixth wealthiest person globally teaches us about innovation, supply chain mastery, and feedback-driven adaptations. Ortega championed the "fast fashion" business model, cutting lead time by controlling the entire supply chain process. Innovatively placing customer feedback at the heart of product development, Ortega proved the supremacy of applying an innovative business model to a traditional industry.

To absorb their wisdom, study their journeys, and apply the lessons can cause a significant shift in anyone's approach to wealth creation. While each of these successful individuals had distinct paths, they all exemplify tenacious work ethic, unique perspectives, long-term focus, and an unwavering belief in their vision. By integrating these millionaire mindsets, we could potentially untap a treasure trove of insights leading us towards our unique journey of accruing wealth.

Chapter 12. Sustaining Wealth: Developing Your Millionaire Legacy

Starting with a life of opulence isn't usually the journey of self-made millionaires. It is, however, one adorned by riches they've personally accrued through the sheer force of their determination, grit and groundbreaking strategies. While a section of world's millionaires inherit their wealth, a surprising majority build it from scratch. And among this majority, an inspiring subset manages to not only amass a fortune but to sustain and grow it, thereby creating a legacy that can benefit generations to come. For those with dreams of becoming part of this unique group, there are specific principles and strategies that form the foundation of their success.

12.1. The Circle of Wealth Generation

Wealth generation among millionaires is not a linear process. It's cyclical, resembling a wheel that turns round, each round marking an increase in wealth. The starting point and the perpetual driver of this cycle is 'value creation'. Millionaires solve problems, innovate, and provide services or products of great value, which in turn generates enormous wealth.

The second stage involves 'wealth protection'. Millionaires are smart about shielding their wealth from unnecessary risks and excessive taxes. They employ advanced tax planning strategies and opt for well-structured insurance plans to safeguard their wealth.

The third stage is 'wealth growth'. Millionaires do not let their money sit idle; it's typically invested in stocks, bonds, real estate, venture capital, or private equity. Good investments not only act as a guard against inflation but they also generate passive income over time.

The final stage is 'wealth distribution' - the carefully planned and organized dispersion of wealth that ensures their legacy endures. They establish wills, trusts, succession plans and philanthropic ventures to distribute their wealth wisely, fostering an enduring legacy.

This cycle repeats, and with each repetition, their wealth expands.

12.2. Cultivating the Mindset: Adaptive and Resilient

Beyond the central framework provided by this cycle, proper wealth management requires a strong mental composition characterized by flexibility and resilience. Despite the common perception that millionaires enjoy a continual and unstinting upsurge of success, they actually face numerous setbacks. Market crashes, poor investment returns, and even personal failures mark their journeys. The true differentiator, however, is their resilience.

They perceive failures as opportunities to learn and adapt. For sustaining wealth, the wealth mindset evolves with the changing financial landscape. They stay updated about new investment opportunities, changes in tax codes, or transitions in the economy and adapt their wealth growth strategies accordingly.

12.3. Establishing Frameworks: Practical Steps

Wealth protection, growth, and distribution need strategic planning and careful execution, encapsulated in these key steps:

1. Creating a financial safety net: Millionaires always maintain a pool of easily accessible funds for emergencies. They ensure their wealth is secured against market downturns and personal emergencies.

2. Diverse investments: They diversify their investment portfolio. Their investments span multiple asset classes, including stocks, bonds, real estate, and more, across different geographical locations and industries. This diversification protects them from severe losses.

3. Fostering wealth creation spaces: Millionaires often invest in new businesses and ventures. By doing so, not only do they get a financial return, but they also create more jobs and, with that, more wealth in the economy.

4. Regular audits: They regularly monitor their wealth. Regular audits reveal how well their protective measures function, guide adjustments to their investment portfolios, and ensure their wealth continues to grow.

5. Planning for transition: They have well-structured wills or trusts, which ensure the smooth transition of wealth, often even planning transitions several generations into the future.

12.4. Building a Lasting Legacy: Philanthropy and Succession

Beyond personal wealth, self-made millionaires are often dedicated to philanthropic causes. They build hospitals, schools, and fund scholarships, transforming their personal wealth into societal wealth. Such philanthropic ventures are not spontaneous acts of generosity; they are the result of careful planning and form an integral part of their wealth distribution strategy.

Additionally, they also care about the succession of their wealth. They do not simply pass on their wealth; they pass on the ethics, values, and skills that accompany wealth generation to the next generation. This helps ensure that the wealth they've amassed provides a lasting and positive impact.

12.5. Conclusion

Sustaining wealth requires a strategic mindset that constantly seeks opportunities, mitigates risks, and adapts to changing circumstances. It is not sufficient to generate wealth; one must protect, grow and distribute it efficiently to leave a lasting legacy. The journey of wealth creation is demanding but richly rewarding. When navigated wisely, it leads not only to monetary riches but to an empowering legacy, one that is marked by societal progress and personal achievement.

Remember, the journey of a thousand miles begins with one step. And achieving the millionaire's mindset is that crucial first step towards a world of endless possibilities, financial freedom, and an enduring legacy. Let this knowledge be your guide as you start your own unique journey towards affluence and financial independence.

www.ingramcontent.com/pod-product-compliance
Lightning Source LLC
Chambersburg PA
CBHW060858260726
48661CB00008B/3340